HEALING THE
BROKENHEARTED

HEALING THE BROKENHEARTED

Experience Restoration
Through the Power of God's Word

JOYCE MEYER

WARNER
Faith

NEW YORK   BOSTON   NASHVILLE

Unless otherwise indicated, all Scripture quotations are taken from *The Amplified Bible* (AMP). *The Amplified Bible, Old Testament* copyright © 1965, 1987 by The Zondervan Corporation. *The Amplified New Testament,* copyright © 1954, 1958, 1987 by The Lockman Foundation. Used by permission.

Warner Books Edition
Copyright © 1997 by Joyce Meyer
Life In the Word, Inc.
P.O. Box 655
Fenton, Missouri 63026
All rights reserved.

Warner Faith

Time Warner Book Group
1271 Avenue of the Americas, New York, NY 10020
Visit our Web site at www.twbookmark.com.

The Warner Faith name and logo are registered trademarks of Warner Books.

Printed in the United States of America

First Warner Faith Printing: February 2003
10   9   8   7   6   5   4   3   2

ISBN: 0-446-69156-9
LCCN: 2002115544

CONTENTS

∽

Contents

HEALING THE BROKENHEARTED

Introduction:
The Word of God

❦ He sends forth His word and heals them and
rescues them from the pit and destruction.

*T*he Word of God heals us and rescues us. It also changes
us and our lives.

The Word of God will change *you*.

In Psalm 1:1–3 David wrote that the person who
meditates on the Word day and night will become
firmly planted like a tree, and that everything he does will
prosper.

To be firmly planted is to be stable. You can be stable,
and everything you do can prosper. The way to do that is
by meditating on the Word of God.

1

To meditate on the Word means to roll it over and over in your mind, to ponder and think on it, and to mutter it to yourself, as the Lord commanded His servant Joshua:

❤ This Book of the Law shall not depart out of your mouth, but you shall meditate on it day and night, that you may observe and do according to all that is written in it. For then you shall make your way prosperous, and then you shall deal wisely and have good success.

JOSHUA 1:8

In Deuteronomy 30:14 we are told, ❤ *"But the word is very near you, in your mouth and in your mind and in your heart, so that you can do it."*

In Isaiah 55:11 the Lord promises us, ❤ *"So shall My word be that goes forth out of My mouth: it shall not return to Me void [without producing any effect, useless], but it shall accomplish that which I please and purpose, and it shall prosper in the thing for which I sent it."*

In 2 Corinthians 3:18 the Apostle Paul teaches us that as we behold the glory of the Lord, in His Word, we are transformed or changed. Part of beholding the glory of the Lord is seeing the glorious plan that He has for us and believing it.

God loves us, and He has a good plan, a glorious plan, for our lives. In the first chapter of Ephesians, Paul says that God devised the entire plan of salvation through Christ in order to satisfy the intense love with which He loved us.

That means God loves you, and He has a wonderful, glorious plan for you and for your life. You need to believe that and confess it.

The devil has tried to ruin God's plan. He has labored all of your life to make you feel worthless. Why? Because he does not want you ever to believe that you are loved dearly by God. Satan knows that hearing the Word of God over and over and allowing it to become part of your inner life, part of your thought system, will change you. And he does not want that to happen.

That is why I have written this book. It contains Scriptures that I believe will change your self-image, thus changing both your present and future.

According to the Bible, you are created in God's image. (GENESIS 1:27.) Believing what God says about you changes your attitude and opinion of yourself. Ask yourself, "What do I think of myself? What is my opinion of myself?" Then ask yourself, "What does God think of me? What is God's opinion of me?"

What God thinks and says about you is found in His Word. The Scripture confessions in this book will bring you into agreement with God instead of with the enemy. Perhaps the devil has lied to you all of your life, and you have believed him. Now it is time to believe God.

In John 17:17, Jesus said that God's Word is Truth, and in John 8:32 He said that it is the Truth that will set us free. Not only will the Word of God, the Word of Truth, set us free, it will also change our very outlook and nature. That is why you need to read it, study it, and meditate on it, allowing it to get down on the inside of you.

In Christ you can be confident, full of joy, an overcomer, faithful, a friend of God, one who seeks God's face.[1]

Confess over yourself what God says about you in His Word. As you do so, God will begin to work in your life. He will change you from being brokenhearted, wounded,

1. Based on the song, "I Will Change Your Name," words and music by B. J. Butler © Mercy Publishing. Used by permission.

4

and afraid to being His faithful friend whom He loves and who loves Him very much.

In Isaiah 61:1–3 we read:

❤ The Spirit of the Lord God is upon me, because the Lord has anointed and qualified me to preach the Gospel of good tidings to the meek, the poor, and afflicted; He has sent me to bind up and heal the brokenhearted, to proclaim liberty to the [physical and spiritual] captives and the opening of the prison and of the eyes to those who are bound.

To proclaim the acceptable year of the Lord [the year of His favor] and the day of vengeance of our God, to comfort all who mourn.

To grant [consolation and joy] to those who mourn in Zion—to give them an ornament (a garland or diadem) of beauty instead of ashes, the oil of joy instead of mourning, the garment [expressive] of praise instead of a heavy, burdened, and failing spirit—that they may be called oaks of righteousness [lofty, strong, and

magnificent, distinguished for uprightness,
justice, and right standing with God], the
planting of the Lord, that He may be glorified.

Yes, God is changing you. He is changing your character. He is changing your life. God loves you. You are a special person. The enemy does not want you to feel loved. But God does.

In the following pages you will learn not only how to be assured of the love of God, but also how to be sure of your future, how to know your righteousness (who you are in Christ), and how to overcome the fear that would rob you of all of the blessings which God desires to pour out upon you as part of the wonderful life He has planned for you.

God bless you as you learn to speak forth His Word that will not return to Him void but will accomplish His will and purpose in your life!

1

❧

Experiencing
the Love of God

❤ Yet amid all these things we are more than
conquerors and gain a surpassing victory through
Him Who loved us.

For I am persuaded beyond doubt (am sure) that
neither death nor life, nor angels nor principalities, nor things impending and threatening nor
things to come, nor powers,

Nor height nor depth, nor anything else in all
creation will be able to separate us from the love
of God which is in Christ Jesus our Lord.

ROMANS 8:37–39

*I*n this passage the Apostle Paul assures us that regardless of what may come against us in this life, overwhelming victory is ours through Christ Who loved us enough to give His life for us.

In John 3:16 Jesus Himself says, ❤ *"For God so greatly loved and dearly prized the world that He [even] gave up His only begotten (unique) Son, so that whoever believes in (trusts in, clings to, relies on) Him shall not perish (come to destruction, be lost) but have eternal (everlasting) life."*

Jesus loves you, personally, so much that He would have given His life for you, even if you had been the only person on earth.

John the Beloved Disciple tells us that ❤ *"there is no fear in love [dread does not exist], but full-grown (complete, perfect) love turns fear out of doors and expels every trace of terror! For fear brings with it the thought of punishment, and [so] he who is afraid has not reached the full maturity of love [is not yet grown into love's complete perfection]"* (1 JOHN 4:18).

When we have fear in our hearts, that is a sign that we still lack the knowledge of how much God loves us.

If you know the magnitude of God's love, it will cause all of your fears to fade away.

In John 16:27 Jesus said, ❤ *"For the Father Himself [tenderly] loves you because you have loved Me and have believed that I came out from the Father."*

Is it difficult for you to believe that God cares so much about you?

For many years I was unable to receive God's love for me because I thought I had to be worthy of His love. But now I know He loves me, even though I still have imperfections.

In John 14:21 Jesus reminds us, ❤ *"The person who has My commands and keeps them is the one who [really] loves Me; and whoever [really] loves Me will be loved by My Father, and I [too] will love him and will show (reveal, manifest) Myself to him. [I will let Myself be clearly seen by him and make Myself real to him.]"*

Jesus wants to make Himself real to *you*.

Obedience is a fruit of true love, but you will never be able to love God enough to obey Him unless you first receive His love for you. You cannot earn it. You cannot buy it with good works, or purchase it with good behavior.

God's love is a free gift; it is unconditional. It comes to

us through the sacrifice that Jesus made when He died for us on the cross.

Receive God's love right now. Sit in His presence and say, "I believe You love me, Lord, and I receive Your love."

In 1 John 4:19 we read, ♥ *"We love Him, because He first loved us."* Perhaps you have been going about it backwards as I did for so many years. You may be trying to love God enough and do enough so He will then love you in return. But look at 1 John 4:19 again, ♥ **"We love Him, because He first loved us."**

David was confident of God's love when he said in Psalm 36:7, ♥ *"How precious is Your steadfast love, O God! The children of men take refuge and put their trust under the shadow of Your wings."*

I would like to share with you passages of Psalm 139. David had a unique way of communicating with God, and we would do well to follow his example. Confess with your mouth the words of this psalm:

> ♥ O Lord, you have examined my heart and know everything about me. You know when I sit or stand. When far away you know my every thought. You chart the path ahead of me, and tell

me where to stop and rest. Every moment, you know where I am. You know what I am going to say before I even say it. You both precede and follow me, and place your hand of blessing on my head.

This is too glorious, too wonderful to believe! I can never be lost to your Spirit! I can never get away from my God!. . . .

How precious it is, Lord, to realize that you are thinking about me constantly! I can't even count how many times a day your thoughts turn towards me. And when I waken in the morning, you are still thinking of me!

PSALM 139:1–7,17,18 TLB

This is powerful!

The Prophet Isaiah tells us that God is waiting to be good to us: ❤ *"And therefore the Lord [earnestly] waits [expecting, looking, and longing] to be gracious to you; and therefore He lifts Himself up, that He may have mercy on you and show loving-kindness to you. For the Lord is a God of*

11

justice. Blessed (happy, fortunate, to be envied) are all those who [earnestly] wait for Him, who expect and look and long for Him [for His victory, His favor, His love, His peace, His joy, and His matchless, unbroken companionship]!" (ISAIAH 30:18).

Think about that, God wants to spend time with you because He loves you and because you are special to Him.

God loves you so much that He numbers and records your wanderings. He puts your tears in a bottle, and writes them in His book. (PSALM 56:8.)

In John 14:18, Jesus told His disciples, ❤ *"I will not leave you as orphans [comfortless, desolate, bereaved, forlorn, helpless]; I will come [back] to you."*

In Psalm 27:10, David wrote, ❤ *"Although my father and my mother have forsaken me, yet the Lord will take me up [adopt me as His child]."*

Perhaps you are lacking the natural love that every person desires and seeks; perhaps even your own family has forsaken you. God wants you to know today that His love for you is so strong, so mighty, and so powerful, that it will override the loss of any other person's love. Let Him comfort you and heal your broken heart.

You have been adopted into the family of God. You are His child, and He loves you.

In Ephesians 3:17–19 the Apostle Paul prayed for you and me:

❤ "May Christ through your faith [actually] dwell (settle down, abide, make His permanent home) in your hearts! May you be rooted deep in love and founded securely on love,

That you may have the power and be strong to apprehend and grasp with all the saints [God's devoted people, the experience of that love] what is the breadth and length and height and depth [of it];

[That you may really come] to know [practically, through experience for yourselves] the love of Christ, which far surpasses mere knowledge [without experience]; that you may be filled [through all your being] unto all the fullness of God [may have the richest measure of the divine Presence, and become a body wholly filled and flooded with God Himself]!

Yes, God loves you, and He is watching over you. He keeps an eye on you all the time. Isaiah 49:16 says that He has a picture of you imprinted and tattooed on the palm of each of His hands.

In John 15:9 (TLB), Jesus said, ❤ " *'I have loved you even as the Father has loved me. Live within my love.'* "

How much does God love you?

❤ "No one has greater love [no one has shown stronger affection] than to lay down (give up) his own life for his friends" (JOHN 15:13).

No one has greater love for you than that.

Jesus wants to be your Friend. He laid down His life for you to show you how much He loves you.

In Romans 5:6 Paul reminds us: ❤ *"While we were yet in weakness [powerless to help ourselves], at the fitting time Christ died for (in behalf of) the ungodly."*

At just the right time, God showed His great love for us by sending Christ to die for us while we were still sinners.

Then in verse 7, Paul goes on to say: ❤ *"Now it is an extraordinary thing for one to give his life even for an upright man, though perhaps for a noble and lovable and generous benefactor someone might even dare to die."*

Finally, in verse 8 Paul concludes: ❤ *"But God shows and clearly proves His [own] love for us by the fact that while we were still sinners, Christ (the Messiah, the Anointed One) died for us."*

Oh, my friend, God loves you so very much. The Holy Spirit is trying to reveal God's love to you. Open your heart and receive the love of God. He accepts you where you are. He never rejects you and never condemns you. (JOHN 3:18.)

In Ephesians 1:6 (KJV) Paul writes that we are made acceptable to God through the Beloved, the Lord Jesus Christ. Our own ability to be perfect is not what makes us acceptable. It is only through Christ that we are made righteous enough to come to the Father.

❤ *"So overflowing is his kindness towards us,"* the Bible says in Ephesians 1:7 (TLB), *"that he [God] took away all our sins through the blood of his Son, by whom we are saved; and he has showered down upon us the richness of his grace—for how well he understands us and knows what is best for us at all times."*

And in Isaiah 54:10 we are told: ❤ *"For though the mountains should depart and the hills be shaken or removed, yet My love and kindness shall not depart from you, nor shall My covenant of peace and completeness be removed, says the Lord, Who has compassion on you."*

In 1 Corinthians 1:9 Paul reminds us that ❤ *"God is faithful (reliable, trustworthy, and therefore ever true to His promise, and He can be depended on). . . ."* He has promised that He will never reject you as long as you believe in Christ, He has also promised that He will love you, and He keeps His promises.

In John 17:9,10 Jesus Himself said that He is praying for you because you belong to Him. You were given to Him by God, and He is glorified in you.

God loves you. Receive that love.

Confess with the psalmist David:

❤ "Bless (affectionately, gratefully praise) the Lord, O my soul; and all that is [deepest] within me, bless His holy name!

Bless (affectionately, gratefully praise) the Lord, O my soul, and forget not [one of] all His benefits—

Who forgives [every one of] all your iniquities, Who heals [each one of] all your diseases,

Who redeems your life from the pit and
corruption, Who beautifies, dignifies, and
crowns you with loving kindness and tender
mercy.

PSALM 103:1–4

In *The Living Bible* version of verses 5, 6, 8, 11–13, 17
David says of the Lord:

❤ "He fills my life with good things! My youth is
renewed like the eagle's! He gives justice to all
who are treated unfairly. . . .

He is merciful and tender toward those who
don't deserve it; he is slow to get angry and full
of kindness and love. He never bears a grudge,
nor remains angry forever . . . for his mercy
toward those who fear and honor him is as great
as the height of the heavens above the earth. He
has removed our sins as far away from us as the
east is from the west. He is like a father to us,
tender and sympathetic to those who reverence
him. . . .

. . . the loving kindness of the Lord is from everlasting to everlasting. . . .

Again, David tells us in Psalm 32:10 (TLB): ❤ "*. . . abiding love surrounds those who trust in the Lord.*" And in Psalm 34:1–8 (TLB) he writes:

❤ I will praise the Lord no matter what happens. I will constantly speak of his glories and grace. I will boast of all his kindness to me. Let all who are discouraged take heart. Let us praise the Lord together, and exalt his name.

For I cried to him and he answered me! He freed me from all my fears. Others too were radiant at what he did for them. Theirs was no downcast look of rejection! This poor man cried to the Lord—and the Lord heard him and saved him out of his troubles. For the Angel of the Lord guards and rescues all who reverence him.

Oh, put God to the test and see how kind he is! See for yourself the way his mercies shower down on all who trust in him.

Peter tells us that love covers a multitude of sins. (1 PETER 4:8.) God's love is covering you. Live under that covering. Let it bless your life. Confess over and over, many times a day, "God loves me."

Meditate upon the Scriptures in this chapter. This obedient action on your part will help you receive from the Lord what He desires to give you—the assurance of His abundant and abiding love.

2

❧

Being Assured
of Your Future

Now I would like to share with you some Scriptures about the great future that God has planned for you. I want you to know that you are valuable and that God had a special purpose in mind when He created you.

In the song titled, "I Have a Destiny," the composer states that he has a destiny he knows he will fulfill, one that was predestined for him by God Who chose him and Who is working mightily through Him by the power of His Spirit. It ends with the stirring confession, "I have a destiny, and it's not an empty wish for I know I was born for such a time, for such a time, for such a time as this."[1]

1. © 1993 People of Destiny (Admin. by WORD Music) All Rights Reserved. Used by permission.

What about you? How do you foresee your future?

God wants you to be full of hope, and the devil wants you to be hopeless. God wants you to expect good things to happen in your life every day. Satan also wants you to expect, but he wants you to expect doom and devastation.

The writer of Proverbs 15:15 says, ❤ *"All the days of the desponding and afflicted are made evil [by anxious thoughts and forebodings], but he who has a glad heart has a continual feast [regardless of circumstances]."*

Evil forebodings are simply expecting bad things to happen before they do. This Scripture clearly states that it is through these evil forebodings that our days end up filled with affliction.

In Psalm 27:13, David writes: ❤ *"[What, what would have become of me] had I not believed that I would see the Lord's goodness in the land of the living!"* In the next verse he exhorts us, *"Wait and hope for and expect the Lord; be brave and of good courage and let your heart be stout and enduring. Yes, wait for and hope for and expect the Lord."*

In Jeremiah 29:11 the Lord reveals His intentions toward us: ❤ *"For I know the thoughts and plans that I have for you, says the Lord, thoughts and plans for welfare and peace and not for evil, to give you hope in your final outcome."*

Remember, the devil wants you hopeless. He wants you to look hopeless, think hopeless, talk hopeless, and act hopeless.

But listen to these powerful words written by David in Psalm 42:11: ❤ *"Why are you cast down, O my inner self? And why should you moan over me and be disquieted within me? Hope in God and wait expectantly for Him, for I shall yet praise Him, Who is the help of my countenance, and my God."*

Having Scriptures like this hidden in your heart will help you to be full of hope and joyful expectation. You will look hopeful, think hopeful, talk hopeful, and act hopeful.

In Romans 5:5 the Apostle Paul tells us that, ❤ *"Such hope never disappoints or deludes or shames us, for God's love has been poured out in our hearts through the Holy Spirit Who has been given to us."*

In other words, we know that God loves us because the Holy Spirit teaches us so. We put our hope in God because we are sure that He loves us and has a great future planned for us. And when our hope and expectation are in Him, we never end up disappointed, deluded, or shamed.

In Psalm 84:11 (KJV) we read, ❤ *"For the Lord God is a sun and shield: the Lord will give grace and glory: no good thing will he withhold from them that walk uprightly."*

In Philippians 1:6, Paul assures us, ❤ *"And I am convinced and sure of this very thing, that He Who began a good work in you will continue until the day of Jesus Christ [right up to the time of His return], developing [that good work] and perfecting and bringing it to full completion in you."*

In Ephesians 2:10 Paul explains the reason for his great assurance:

> ❤ For we are God's [own] handiwork (His workmanship), recreated in Christ Jesus, [born anew] that we may do those good works which God predestined (planned beforehand) for us [taking paths which He prepared ahead of time], that we should walk in them [living the good life which He prearranged and made ready for us to live].

Now you may be asking yourself, "If God has such a good plan for me, when am I going to see it?"

The answer is written in Ecclesiastes 3:17: ❤ *". . . for there is a time [appointed] for every matter and purpose and for every work."*

24

God will bring to pass His plan and purpose for you in His own time. Your part is simply to do as Peter suggests, which is to humble yourself under the mighty hand of God that in due time he may exalt you. (1 PETER 5:6.)

In Habakkuk 2:2 the Lord gave His prophet a vision of His plan for the future, commanding him to write it down so that others could read it. But in the next verse He went on to say, ❤ " *'But these things I plan won't happen right away. Slowly, steadily, surely, the time approaches when the vision will be fulfilled. If it seems slow, do not despair, for these things will surely come to pass. Just be patient! They will not be overdue a single day!'"* (HABAKKUK 2:3 TLB).

The writer of Hebrews 6:18,19 (NAS) tells us that these things were written so that ❤ *". . . we may have strong encouragement, we who have fled for refuge in laying hold of the hope set before us. This hope we have as an anchor of the soul, a hope both sure and steadfast and one which enters within the veil."*

And Paul says that ❤ *". . . all things work together for good to them that love God, to them who are the called according to his purpose"* (ROMANS 8:28 KJV). Later, in his letter to the church at Ephesus, Paul reminds us that we have purpose, saying, ❤ *"Now to Him Who, by (in consequence of) the [action of His] power that is at work within us, is able to [carry out His purpose and] do superabundantly, far over and above all that we [dare] ask or think [infinitely beyond our highest prayers, desires, thoughts, hopes, or dreams]—"* (EPHESIANS 3:20).

God wants you to be full of hope because He is ready to do even greater things than you are able to hope for. However, if you are hopeless—as the devil wants you to be—then you are not doing the part that God has asked you to do, which is put your hope and expectation in Him, believing He has a good plan for your life and trusting that plan is in the process of being worked out.

In Ephesians 1:11 Paul says of the Lord Jesus Christ, ❤ *"In Him we also were made [God's] heritage (portion) and we obtained an inheritance; for we had been foreordained (chosen and appointed beforehand) in accordance with His purpose, Who works out everything in agreement with the counsel and design of His [own] will."*

Remember God's command to His servant in Joshua 1:8: ❤ *"This Book of the Law shall not depart out of your mouth, but you shall meditate on it day and night, that you may observe and do according to all that is written in it. For then you* shall make your way prosperous, and then you shall deal wisely and have good success."

Remember also Deuteronomy 30:14 which says, ❤ *"But the word is very near you, in your mouth and in your mind and in your heart, so that you can do it."*

In Isaiah 55:11 the Lord shows us how confessing His Word will help bring His purposes to pass in our lives: ❤ *"So shall My word be that goes forth out of My mouth: it shall not return to Me void [without producing any effect, useless], but it shall accomplish that which I please and purpose, and it shall prosper in the thing for which I sent it."*

Give your mouth to God, let it become His mouth. Begin to speak His Word, because He has a good future, a good purpose, and a good plan for you. Speak in agreement with God, not with the enemy.

Remember, each of us has a divine destiny.

What do you think you will be like in the future? The devil wants you to think that you are getting worse all the time instead of better. He wants you to meditate on how far you have to go, not how far you have come.

Do you get frustrated with yourself, feeling that you are never going to change? Be hopeful, God is changing you all the time. His Word is working mightily in you.

Deuteronomy 7:22 reminds us that He helps us overcome our enemies little by little.

In 2 Corinthians 3:18 Paul says that as we behold the Lord in His Word, we are constantly being transfigured or changed into His image and that it happens ❤ *"from one degree of glory to another."*

Then in Romans 12:2 we read we are transformed by the entire renewal of our minds and by these new thoughts, ideals, and attitudes, we prove for ourselves what is ❤ *"the good and acceptable and perfect will of God, even the thing which is good and acceptable and perfect [in His sight for you]."*

In Colossians 1:27 Paul states that the mystery of the ages is Christ in us, the hope of glory. Your heavenly Father sees you glorified. He has such a vision of you in a glorified state that He sent His Spirit to dwell in you to make sure it comes to pass.

I define the word "glory" as the manifestation of all of the excellencies of our God. Put your hope in Him and believe that all these Scriptures are for you.

Learn to make positive, faith-filled, Word-based confessions. Say out loud, "I am being transformed into God's image from one degree of glory to another." (2 CORINTHIANS 3:18) "Christ in me is my hope of being more glorious. The Spirit of God is transforming me daily, little by little. My life has purpose. God has a good plan for me."

Remember, according to Romans 4:17 (KJV), we serve a God Who *"calleth"* those things which be not as though they were.

What does God say about us in His Word?

❤ . . . you are a chosen race, a royal priesthood,
a dedicated nation, [God's] own purchased,
special people, that you may set forth the
wonderful deeds and display the virtues and
perfections of Him Who called you out of
darkness into His marvelous light.

1 PETER 2:9

God intends to display or manifest, to bring out into the open where they can be seen, the wonderful deeds, virtues, and perfections that He has planned for you.

Learn to say, "I am called out of darkness into God's glorious light."

Having a poor self-image is darkness. Disliking your-self is darkness. Thinking you have no value or worth is darkness.

In Malachi 3:17 we learn we are the Lord's jewels, His special possession, His peculiar treasure. Yes, you are valu-able, and you have a purpose. You have a destiny. God has a great plan for your life. You have a part to play in history, but you must believe it to receive it.

You may say, "But Joyce, I have failed so many times. I have made so many mistakes, I know I have disappointed God."

In Philippians 3:13, 14 Paul admitted that he had not yet arrived at perfection, but he also confessed that he was not giving up:

> ❤ I do not consider, brethren, that I have captured and made it my own [yet]; but one thing I do [it is my one aspiration]: forgetting what lies behind and straining forward to what lies ahead,
>
> I press on toward the goal to win the [supreme and heavenly] prize to which God in Christ Jesus is calling us upward.

God has a good plan for your life. Do not live in the past. Hear the Word of the Lord as recorded in Isaiah 43:18, 19:

❤ Do not [earnestly] remember the former things; neither consider the things of old.

Behold, I am doing a new thing! Now it springs forth; do you not perceive and know it and will you not give heed to it? I will even make a way in the wilderness and rivers in the desert.

Finally, listen to what God is saying to you in Isaiah 43:25: ❤ *"I, even I, am He Who blots out and cancels your transgressions; for My own sake, and I will not remember your sins."*

God so much wants to see you become all that He has planned for you to be. He wants to see you enjoy to the fullest the good life that He has destined for you. He is willing by His grace and mercy to remove everything that you have done wrong in the past. He has even made provision for all the mistakes you will ever make in the future.

You do not have to live in remorse for the past, nor in fear of the future. God is willing to help you in any way you need help.

Isaiah 40:31 promises that ❤ "... *those who wait for the Lord [who expect, look for, and hope in Him] shall change and renew their strength and power; they shall lift their wings and mount up [close to God] as eagles [mount up to the sun]; they shall run and not be weary, they shall walk and not faint or become tired."*

What a wonderful assurance of God's abiding love and His miraculous provision for every need you will face in the days ahead.

Armed with His marvelous promises and His precious plans, face the future with hope and confidence, assured that what He has promised He is well able to perform. (ROMANS 4:21.)

Don't look back, look ahead. Step out in faith.

Remember, you have a divine destiny to fulfill!

3

❧

KNOWING YOUR
RIGHTEOUSNESS IN CHRIST

Now I would like to share with you some Scriptures about righteousness.

The song, "I Have Been Made The Righteousness Of God," speaks of being adopted into God's own family and standing before His throne as a member of royalty, complete in Jesus and a joint-heir with Him, without sin, purchased by His precious blood.[1]

You are the righteousness of God in Jesus Christ, as Paul wrote in 2 Corinthians 5:21: ❤ *"For our sake He [God] made Christ [virtually] to be sin Who knew no sin, so that in and through Him we might become [endued with, viewed as*

1. Words and music by Chris Sellmeyer © 1992 by Life In The Word, Inc.

being in, and examples of] the righteousness of God [what we ought to be, approved and acceptable and in right relationship with Him, by His goodness]."

Psalm 48:10 says of the Lord, ♥ "As is Your name, O God, so is Your praise to the ends of the earth; Your right hand is full of righteousness (rightness and justice)."

God's hand is stretched out to you, full of righteousness.

In 1 Corinthians 1:8 the Apostle Paul assures you that ♥ "He [God] will establish you to the end [keep you steadfast, give you strength, and guarantee your vindication; He will be your warrant against all accusation or indictment so that you will be] guiltless and irreproachable in the day of our Lord Jesus Christ (the Messiah)."

Do you know what that means? That means that God sees you in right standing now. Today, He has you right where He wants you. He stands ready to defend you from the lies of Satan, the accuser of the brethren. (REVELATION 12:10 KJV.)

If you have put your trust in Jesus Christ, God does not see you as guilty. He is willing to prove your innocence.

In the Sermon on the Mount, Jesus told His followers:
❤ *"Blessed and fortunate and happy and spiritually prosperous (in that state in which the born-again child of God enjoys His favor and salvation) are those who hunger and thirst for righteousness (uprightness and right standing with God), for they shall be completely satisfied!"* (MATTHEW 5:6).

According to Jesus, as a born-again child of God, you are entitled to live in a state in which you enjoy God's favor. You have a right to enjoy life. It is God's gift to you.

Begin to confess this statement: "I am the righteousness of God in Jesus Christ."

Perhaps you have taken the burden of trying to make yourself right with God. That is not the way righteousness comes. Righteousness, like salvation, is not a work; it is a gift. Give up your efforts and learn to trust in God to impart to you the righteousness of Christ.

❤ *"Cast your burden on the Lord [releasing the weight of it] and He will sustain you; He will never allow the [consistently] righteous to be moved (made to slip, fall, or fail)"* (PSALM 55:22).

In Romans 4:1–3 Paul speaks of the righteousness of Abraham:

❤ . . . what shall we say about Abraham, our forefather humanly speaking—[what did he] find out? [How does this affect his position, and what was gained by him?]

For if Abraham was justified (established as just by acquittal from guilt) by good works [that he did, then] he has grounds for boasting. But not before God!

For what does the Scripture say? Abraham believed in (trusted in) God, and it was credited to his account as righteousness (right living and right standing with God).

Then in verses 23 and 24 Paul goes on to point out:

❤ "But [the words], It was credited to him, were written not for his sake alone,

But [they were written] for our sakes too. [Righteousness, standing acceptable to God] will be granted and credited to us also who believe in

(trust in, adhere to, and rely on) God, Who
raised Jesus our Lord from the dead.

In other words, what Paul is telling us here is that we
receive righteousness through believing, not doing.

When we believe in Jesus Christ, God views us as righteous. Literally, He makes a decision to see us as right with
Him because of the blood of Jesus. He is the sovereign God,
and He has the right to make that decision if He chooses.

In the first verse of the next chapter, Paul summarizes
his point: ❤ *"Therefore, since we are justified (acquitted, declared righteous, and given a right standing with God) through
faith, let us [grasp the fact that we] have [the peace of reconciliation to hold and to enjoy] peace with God through our Lord
Jesus Christ (the Messiah, the Anointed One)"* (ROMANS 5:1).

Righteousness does not come through our own feeble
works; it comes through the finished work of Jesus.

In Psalm 37:25 David wrote: ❤ *"I have been young and
now am old, yet have I not seen the [uncompromisingly] righteous forsaken or their seed begging bread."*

I believe that, as parents, if we can take hold of our
righteous position with God through Christ, our children
can adopt that righteousness.

Children who are raised by parents who feel guilty, condemned, and worthless generally adopt those feelings from their parents.

Likewise, if parents understand and believe that God loves them, that they are special to Him, that God has a good plan for their lives, that they have been made righteous through the blood of Christ, then the children living under the covering of that truth will be affected by their parents' faith and will receive Jesus and all of His promises as their own.

Proverbs 20:7 tells us that ❤ *"the righteous man walks in his integrity; blessed (happy, fortunate, enviable) are his children after him."*

And in Psalm 37:39 we read: ❤ *"But the salvation of the [consistently] righteous is of the Lord; He is their Refuge and secure Stronghold in the time of trouble."*

The Lord is on your side. His Word is true, and it promises peace, righteousness, security, and triumph over opposition.

Learn to confess this promise from the Lord, found in Isaiah 54:17: ❤ *". . . no weapon that is formed against you shall prosper, and every tongue that shall rise against you in judgment you shall show to be in the wrong, This [peace, righteousness, security, triumph over opposition] is the heritage of the servants of the Lord [those in whom the ideal Servant of the Lord is reproduced]; this is the righteousness or the vindication which they obtain from Me [this is that which I impart to them as their justification], says the Lord."*

In Psalm 34:15 David tells us:

❤ The eyes of the Lord are toward the [uncompromisingly] righteous and His ears are open to their cry.

That literally means that God is watching you and listening to you because He loves you.

Then in verses 17, 19 and 22 David goes on to say:

❤ When the righteous cry for help, the Lord hears, and delivers them out of all their distress and troubles. . . .

Many evils confront the [consistently] righteous, but the Lord delivers him out of them all. . . .

The Lord redeems the lives of His servants, and
none of those who take refuge and trust in Him
shall be condemned or held guilty.

From the time you receive Jesus as Savior, you are
growing in Him. You might say that you are on a journey.
While you are on your way, you will make some mistakes.
Your performance may not be perfect, but if your heart is
perfect toward the Lord, I believe He counts you as perfect
while you are making the trip.

In Isaiah 54:14 the Lord declares: ❤ *"You shall establish yourself in righteousness (rightness, in conformity with
God's will and order): you shall be far from even the thought of
oppression or destruction, for you shall not fear, and from terror,
for it shall not come near you."*

Proverbs 28:1 says that the uncompromisingly righteous are as bold as a lion. When you know that you are
righteous through Christ, when you have true revelation in
this area, then you will not live in fear and terror, because
righteousness produces boldness:

❤ For we do not have a High Priest Who is
unable to understand and sympathize and have a

shared feeling with our weaknesses and
infirmities and liability to the assaults of
temptation, but One Who has been tempted
in every respect as we are, yet without
sinning.

Let us then fearlessly and confidently and boldly
draw near to the throne of grace (the throne of
God's unmerited favor to us sinners), that we
may receive mercy [for our failures] and find
grace to help in good time for every need
[appropriate help and well-timed help, coming
just when we need it].

HEBREWS 4:15, 16

We may approach God's throne of grace boldly, not
because of our perfection but because of His: ❤ *"Therefore, since we are now justified (acquitted, made righteous, and
brought into right relationship with God) by Christ's blood, how
much more [certain is it that] we shall be saved by Him from the
indignation and wrath of God"* (ROMANS 5:9).

Perhaps all of your life you have wondered, "What is
wrong with me?"

If so, I announce unto you good news: **you have been made righteous!**

Now there is something **right** about you.

This is something I encourage people to confess all the time: "I may not be where I need to be, but thank God, I'm not where I used to be. I'm okay, and I'm on my way."

Remember, change is a process, and you are in that process. While you are changing, God sees you as righteous.

You **are** righteous. It is the state that God has placed you in through the blood of Jesus.

The changes occurring in your life are a manifestation of the righteous position that God has already given you through faith.

Glory to God!

This is powerful!

As you receive God's love and righteousness, you will be delivered from insecurity and the fear of rejection.

Right now, stop and declare, "I am the righteousness of God in Jesus Christ." I encourage you to begin to confess that truth several times every day.

In Romans 14:17 (KJV), the Apostle Paul tells us that ♥ *"the kingdom of God is not meat and drink; but righteousness, and peace, and joy in the Holy Ghost."* Righteousness leads to peace, and peace leads to joy.

If you have been lacking peace and joy, perhaps you have been lacking revelation on your righteousness. God does want to bless you, physically and financially.

However, most guilty, condemned people never receive true prosperity. The Bible teaches us that the righteous, those who know they are righteous, prosper, and are kept safe.

Do you know what the Lord says about you? In Psalm 1:3, He says the man who delights in the law of the Lord and His instructions is like a tree planted by the rivers of water that brings forth its fruit in its season. Your leaf shall not wither, and everything you do shall prosper and succeed.

Meditate upon your right standing with God, not upon everything that is wrong with you.

As we have seen, in Joshua 1:8, ♥ *"This Book of the Law shall not depart out of your mouth, but you shall meditate on it day and night, that you may observe and do according to all that is written in it. For then you shall make your way prosperous, and then you shall deal wisely and have good success."*

Remember that Psalm 1:2, 3 says that when you have habitually meditated on the Word of God day and night, then you will be like that tree firmly planted that brings forth fruit and prospers in everything it does.

Meditate on the Word and speak the Word. When Satan attacks your mind, counterattack with the Word of God. Remember, Jesus defeated the devil by speaking the Word, saying, ❤ *"It is written"* (LUKE 4:4, 8, 10).

Proverbs 18:10 says: ❤ *"The name of the Lord is a strong tower; the [consistently] righteous man [upright and in right standing with God], runs into it and is safe, high [above evil] and strong."*

Psalm 72:7 says that the righteous shall ❤ *"flourish and peace abound till there is a moon no longer."* Accept your righteousness with God so you can begin to flourish in peace.

You may be thinking, "But what about all the terrible things I have done?"

I want to remind you of the words spoken of His people by God as recorded in Hebrews 10:16–18:

❤ This is the agreement (testament, covenant) that I will set up and conclude with them after those days, says the Lord: I will imprint My laws upon their hearts, and I will inscribe them on their minds (on their inmost thoughts and understanding),

. . . their sins and their lawbreaking I will remember no more.

Now where there is absolute remission (forgiveness and cancellation of the penalty) of these [sins and lawbreaking], there is no longer any offering made to atone for sin.

In other words, your sins have been absolutely canceled with the penalty for them. Since Jesus has done such a thorough and complete job, there is nothing you can do to make up for your sins. The only thing you can do that will please God is to accept, by faith, what He wants to freely give you.

Hebrews 10:19,20 says of Jesus that by His sacrifice He has opened up a ❤ *"fresh (new) and living way"* whereby we may be full of freedom and confidence to enter into His presence ❤ *"by the power and virtue"* that is in His blood.

There no longer needs to be a separating veil between you and God.

What glorious news!

You can come in **boldly** and fellowship with God because your sin has been canceled, removed, and forgotten.

Rejoice! You are the righteousness of God in Christ! (2 CORINTHIANS 5:21.)

4

❧

OVERCOMING THE FEAR
IN YOUR LIFE

*D*o you have fears about yourself?

In the song, "Fear Not My Child," the Lord speaks these words of life:

> *"Fear not My child*
> *I'm with you always.*
> *I feel every pain*
> *And I see all your tears.*
> *Fear not My child*
> *I'm with you always.*
> *I know how to take care*
> *of what belongs to Me."*[1]

1. © 1986 Some-O-Dat Music (Admin. by WORD Music) All Rights Reserved. Used by permission.

In 2 Timothy 1:7 the Apostle Paul writes to his young disciple to urge him not to be afraid to exercise his ministry: ❤ *"For God did not give us a spirit of timidity (of cowardice, of craven and cringing and fawning fear), but [He has given us a spirit] of power and of love and of calm and well-balanced mind and discipline and self-control."*

Remember that verse. Memorize it and repeat it every time you are tempted to become anxious and fearful.

Fear is not from God. Satan is the one who wants to fill your heart with fear. God has a plan for your life. Receive His plan by putting your faith in Him. But remember, Satan also has a plan for your life. You receive his plan through fear.

The psalmist David wrote, ❤ *"I sought (inquired of) the Lord and required Him [of necessity and on the authority of His Word], and He heard me, and delivered me from all my fears"* (PSALM 34:4).

Jesus is your Deliverer. As you diligently seek Him, He will deliver you from all your fears. In John 14:27 He told His frightened disciples: ❤ *". . . Do not let your hearts be troubled, neither let them be afraid. [Stop allowing yourselves to be agitated and disturbed; and do not permit yourselves to be fearful and intimidated and cowardly and unsettled]."*

That means that you will need to aggressively take a stand against fear. Make a decision today that you will no longer let a spirit of fear intimate you and dominate your life.

In Psalm 56:3,4 David said of the Lord:

❤ What time I am afraid, I will have confidence in and put my trust and reliance in You.

By [the help of] God I will praise His word; on God I lean, rely, and confidently put my trust; I will not fear. What can man, who is flesh, do to me?

In Isaiah 41:10 the Lord assures His people: ❤ *"Fear not [there is nothing to fear], for I am with you; do not look around you in terror and be dismayed, for I am your God. I will strengthen and harden you to difficulties, yes, I will help you; yes, I will hold you up and retain you with My [victorious] right hand of rightness and justice."*

The writer of Hebrews 13:5 warns against striving for earthly possessions and security, reminding us: ❤ *". . . for He [God] Himself has said, I will not in any way fail you nor give you up nor leave you without support. [I will] not, [I will] not, [I will] not in any degree leave you helpless nor forsake nor let [you] down (relax My hold on you)! [Assuredly not!]"*

Then in verse 6 the writer goes on to say, ❤ *"So we take comfort and are encouraged and confidently and boldly say, the Lord is my Helper; I will not be seized with alarm [I will not fear or dread or be terrified]. What can man do to me?"*

Fear, which is spelled f-e-a-r, stands for **false evidence appearing real**. The enemy wants to tell you that your current situation is evidence that your future will be a failure, but the Bible teaches us that no matter what our present circumstances, no matter how bad things seem, nothing is impossible with God. (MARK 9:17–23.)

In Isaiah 41:13 we are told, ❤ *"For I the Lord thy God will hold thy right hand, saying unto thee, Fear not; I will help thee!"* (KJV). This means that you don't have to be afraid when you bear bad news. Keep your trust in God. He can cause all things to work out for your good.

In Romans 8:28 the Apostle Paul reminds us that all things work together for good to those who love God and who are called according to His design and purpose.

In Isaiah 43:1–3 (TLB) we read: ❤ *"But now the Lord who created you, O Israel, says, Don't be afraid, for I have ran-*

somed you; I have called you by name; you are mine. When you go through deep waters and great trouble, I will be with you. When you go through rivers of difficulty, you will not drown! When you walk through the fire of oppression, you will not be burned up—the flames will not consume you. For I am the Lord your God, your Savior, the Holy One of Israel. . . ."

Learn to confess these Scriptures on fear, out loud. Speak them out in the atmosphere when you are alone. Establish in the spiritual realm that you do not intend to live in fear. By declaring the Word of God, you are serving notice on the devil that you do not intend to lead a life of torment.

Remember, the Bible says that fear has torment. (1 JOHN 4:18 KJV.) Jesus died to deliver us from torment, as we see in Ephesians 3:12, 13, in which Paul tells us that because of our faith in Jesus Christ,

❤ . . . we dare to have the boldness (courage and confidence) of free access (an unreserved approach to God with freedom and without fear).

So I ask you not to lose heart [not to faint or become despondent through fear]. . . .

In Psalm 46:1, 2 we are reminded:

❤ God is our Refuge and Strength [mighty and impenetrable to temptation], a very present and well-proved help in trouble.

Therefore we will not fear, though the earth should change and though the mountains be shaken into the midst of the seas.

In the first chapter of Joshua, God repeatedly encourages Joshua to ❤ *"be strong (confident) and of good courage"* (v. 6), assuring him, ❤ *"the Lord your God is with you wherever you go"* (v. 9). Therefore you need not be afraid. And the Lord's message to you is the same as it was to Joshua.

God is with you. He will never leave you nor forsake you. (HEBREWS 13:5.) He keeps an eye on you at all times. (PSALM 33:18.) He has a picture of you tattooed on the palm of each of His hands. (ISAIAH 49:16.) Therefore, you need not fear. Be strong, be confident, be full of courage, be not afraid.

In Matthew 6:34, in the Sermon on the Mount, Jesus taught His followers: ❤ *"So do not worry or be anxious about tomorrow, for tomorrow will have worries and anxieties of its own. Sufficient for each day is its own trouble."*

In Matthew 8:23–27 we read how the disciples became frightened by the storm at sea: ❤ *"And He said to them, Why are you timid and afraid, O you of little faith? Then He got up and rebuked the winds and the sea, and there was a great and wonderful calm (a perfect peaceableness)"* (verse 26).

In Luke 12:25, 26 (TLB) Jesus asks, ❤ *". . . what's the use of worrying? What good does it do? Will it add a single day to your life? Of course not! And if worry can't even do such little things as that, what's the use of worrying over bigger things?*

"Fear not;" said Isaiah in chapter 54, verse 4 (TLB); ❤ *"you will no longer live in shame. The shame of your youth and the sorrows of widowhood will be remembered no more, for your Creator will be your 'husband.' The Lord of Hosts is his name; he is your Redeemer, the Holy One of Israel, the God of all the earth."*

Then in Isaiah 35:4 we read, ❤ *"Say to those who are of a fearful and hasty heart, Be strong, fear not! Behold, your God will come with vengeance; with the recompense of God He will come and save you."*

Ask God to strengthen you in the inner man, that His might and power may fill you, and that you may not be overcome with the temptation to give in to fear. (EPHE-SIANS 3:16.)

I would like to share with you a great revelation that God has given me concerning fear. When the Lord speaks to us through His Word and says, ❤ *"Fear not,"* He is not commanding us not to feel fear. What He is actually saying is, "When you feel fear, that is, when the devil attacks you with fear, don't back down or run away. Instead, go forward even though you are afraid."

For many years, I thought I was a coward when I felt fearful. Now I have learned that the way to overcome fear is to face it head-on, to confront it, and to press on through it, doing whatever God has spoken to do, even if it must be done while afraid.

In *The Living Bible* version of Psalm 34:4 David said of the Lord, ❤ *"For I cried to him and he answered me! He freed me from all my fears."* And John reminds us, *"There is no fear in love [dread does not exist], but full-grown (complete, perfect) love turns fear out of doors and expels every trace of terror! For fear brings with it the thought of punishment, and [so] he who is afraid has not reached the full maturity of love [is not yet grown into love's complete perfection]"* (1 JOHN 4:18).

Remember, God loves you! And because He loves you

and cares about you with a perfect love, you can live free from fear.

Perhaps you have so many fears in your life at this time that to live free from fear seems like an impossible dream. If so, there is something that you need to remember: God can completely deliver you from any problem, all at once, but He often delivers little by little. Therefore, be encouraged that the Lord is working in you. God has begun a good work in you, and He **will** complete it. (PHILIPPIANS 1:6.)

❤ *"The Lord is my light and my salvation; whom shall I fear?"* asks the psalmist in chapter 27, verse 1 (TLB). ❤ *"When evil men come to destroy me, they will stumble and fall! Yes, though a mighty army marches against me, my heart shall know no fear! I am confident that God will save me."*

In verses 5 and 6 of that same passage David goes on to say that when trouble comes, God will hide him. He will set him on a high rock, out of the reach of all his enemies. Then he says that he will bring the Lord sacrifices and will sing His praises with great joy.

What God did for King David, He will do for you. Put your faith in the Lord. He has the power to deliver you from all fear.

Listen to these words that the Angel of the Lord spoke to Daniel, reassuring him that his prayers had definitely been heard: ❤ *". . . Fear not, Daniel, for from the first day that you set your mind and heart to understand and to humble yourself before your God, your words were heard, and I have come as a consequence of [and in response to] your words"* (DANIEL 10:12).

The devil will try to tell you that God has not heard your prayer and will not answer you. Remember that the Word of God is the sword of the Spirit. (EPHESIANS 6:17.) With the sword of the Word, you defeat the enemy. Hide these Scriptures in your heart, meditate upon them day and night.

Only with the Word of God will you be able to defeat the enemy. Only when you know God's Word will you recognize the lies of Satan. Confess the Word of God, and it will bring you into a place of victory.

Perhaps you are fearful about talking to someone who is in authority over you. Perhaps you have been accused of something and are concerned about what you should say in your own defense. Listen to the words of Jesus in Luke 12:11, 12 (TLB): ❤ *"And when you are brought to trial before . . . rulers and authorities . . . , don't be concerned about what to say in your defense, for the Holy Spirit will give you the right words even as you are standing there."*

When you are tempted to give in to fear, repeat Psalm 23:1–6 (KJV) as your confession of faith in the Lord and His provision for you and His watchful care over you:

❤ The Lord is my shepherd; I shall not want.

He maketh me to lie down in green pastures:
he leadeth me beside the still waters.

He restoreth my soul: he leadeth me in the paths
of righteousness for his name's sake.

Yea, though I walk through the valley of the
shadow of death, I will fear no evil: for thou art
with me; thy rod and thy staff they comfort me.

Thou preparest a table before me in the presence
of mine enemies: thou anointest my head with
oil; my cup runneth over.

Surely goodness and mercy shall follow me all the
days of my life: and I will dwell in the house of
the Lord for ever.

Conclusion: Stand Fast!

❧

*I*n this book, I am sharing with you Scriptures about the love of God, the glorious future He has planned for you, your righteousness in Christ, and freedom from fear.

All of the promises recorded in these Scriptures are your heritage as a servant of the Lord. However, you need to know that the devil will try to steal them from you. He wants you to go back to bondage.

That's why the Apostle Paul tells us in Galatians 5:1 (KJV), ♥ *"Stand fast therefore in the liberty wherewith Christ hath made us free, and be not entangled again with the yoke of bondage."*

Some of the keys to the victorious Christian life are steadfastness, patience, and endurance:

> ♥ Do not, therefore, fling away your fearless confidence, for it carries a great and glorious compensation of reward.

For you have need of steadfast patience and endurance, so that you may perform and fully accomplish the will of God, and thus receive and carry away [and enjoy to the full] what is promised.

HEBREWS 10:35, 36

Your heavenly Father wants you to enjoy fully what was purchased for you by the blood of Jesus Christ. Be determined. Make a decision right now that you will never give up. Confess the Scriptures in the following section until they have become a part of your very being.

Always remember that God loves you, and that there is life in His Word.

SCRIPTURE CONFESSIONS

❦

Introduction: The Word of God*

God sends forth His Word and heals me and rescues me from the pit and destruction. (PSALM 107:20.)

Blessed (happy, fortunate, prosperous, and enviable) am I because I walk and live not in the counsel of the ungodly [following their advice, their plans and purposes], nor stand [submissive and inactive] in the path where sinners walk, nor sit down [to relax and rest] where the scornful [and the mockers] gather.

But my delight and desire are in the law of the Lord, and on His law (the precepts, the instructions, the teachings of God) I habitually meditate (ponder and study) by day and by night.

*Note: The author has personalized the confessions for the reader by paraphrasing the referenced Scriptures in first person.

And I shall be like a tree firmly planted [and tended] by the streams of water, ready to bring forth fruit in season; my leaf also shall not fade or wither; and everything I do shall prosper [and come to maturity]. (PSALM 1:1–3.)

This Book of the Law shall not depart out of my mouth, but I shall meditate on it day and night, that I may observe and do according to all that is written in it. For then I shall make my way prosperous, and then I shall deal wisely and have good success. (JOSHUA 1:8.)

The Word is very near me, in my mouth and in my mind and in my heart, so that I can do it. (DEUTERONOMY 30:14.)

So shall God's Word be that goes forth out of my mouth: it shall not return to Him void [without producing any effect, useless], but it shall accomplish that which He pleases and purposes, and it shall prosper in the thing for which He sent it. (ISAIAH 55:11.)

Because I, with unveiled face, continue to behold [in the Word of God] as in a mirror the glory of the Lord, I am constantly being transfigured into His very own image in ever increasing splendor and from one degree of glory to another; [for this comes] from the Lord [Who is] the Spirit. (2 CORINTHIANS 3:18.)

God's Word is Truth. As I study and meditate on it, I will know the Truth, and the Truth will set me free. (JOHN 17:17; 8:32.)

Chapter 1: The Love of God

Yet amid all these things I am more than a conqueror and gain a surpassing victory through Him Who loves me.

For I am persuaded beyond doubt (am sure) that neither death nor life, nor angels nor principalities, nor things impending and threatening nor things to come, nor powers,

Nor height; nor depth, nor anything else in all creation will be able to separate me from the love of God which is in Christ Jesus my Lord. (ROMANS 8:37–39.)

For God so greatly loved and dearly prized me that He [even] gave up His only begotten (unique) Son for me, so that I who believe in (trust in, cling to, rely on) Him shall not perish (come to destruction, be lost) but have eternal (everlasting) life. (JOHN 3:16.)

The Father Himself [tenderly] loves me because I love Jesus and believe that He came out from the Father. (JOHN 16:27.)

Because I have the commands of Jesus and keep them, I [really] love Jesus; and because I [really] love Jesus, I will be loved by His Father, and Jesus [too] will love me and will show (reveal, manifest) Himself to me. [He will let Himself be clearly seen by me and will make Himself real to me.] (JOHN 14:21.)

I love the Lord, because He first loved me. (1 JOHN 4:19.)

How precious is Your steadfast love, O God! I take refuge and put my trust under the shadow of Your wings. (PSALM 36:7.)

O Lord, You have examined my heart and know everything about me. You know when I sit or stand. When far away You know my every thought. You chart the path ahead of me, and tell me where to stop and rest. Every moment You know where I am. You know what I am going to say before I even say it. You both precede and follow me, and place Your hand of blessing on my head.

This is too glorious, too wonderful to believe! I can never be lost to Your Spirit! I can never get away from You, my God!

How precious it is, Lord, to realize that You are thinking about me constantly! I can't even count how many times a day Your thoughts turn towards me. And when I awaken in the morning, You are still thinking of me! (PSALM 139:1–7, 17, 18 TLB.)

The Lord [earnestly] waits [expecting, looking, and longing] to be gracious to me; and therefore He lifts Himself up, that He may have mercy on me and show lovingkindness to me. For the Lord is a God of justice. Blessed (happy, fortunate, to be envied) am I because I [earnestly] wait for Him, I expect and look and long for Him [for His victory, His favor, His love, His peace, His joy, and His matchless, unbroken companionship]! (ISAIAH 30:18.)

The Lord will not leave me as an orphan [comfortless, desolate, bereaved, forlorn, helpless]; He will come [back] to me. (JOHN 14:18.)

Although my father and my mother may forsake me, yet the Lord will take me up [adopt me as His child]. (PSALM 27:10.)

Christ through my faith [actually] dwells (settles down, abides, makes His permanent home) in my heart! I am rooted deep in love and founded securely on love.

I have the power to be strong to apprehend and grasp with all the saints [God's devoted people, the experience of that love] what is the breadth and length and height and depth [of it].

[I have really come] to know [practically, through experience for myself] the love of Christ, which far surpasses mere knowledge [without experience]; I am filled [through all my being] unto all the fullness of God [I have the richest measure of the divine Presence, and have become a body wholly filled and flooded with God Himself]! (EPHESIANS 3:17–19.)

Jesus loves me even as the Father loves Him; therefore I live within His love. And here is how to measure His love for me—the greatest love is shown when a person lays down his life for his friends. (JOHN 15:9, 13 TLB.)

God shows and clearly proves His [own] love for me by the fact that while I was still a sinner, Christ (the Messiah, the Anointed One) died for me. (ROMANS 5:8.)

So overflowing is the Lord's kindness towards me that He took away all my sins through the blood of His Son, by Whom I am saved, and has showered down upon me the richness of His grace—for how well He understands me and knows what is best for me at all times. (EPHESIANS 1:7 TLB.)

For though the mountains should depart and the hills be shaken or removed, yet God's love and kindness shall not depart from me, nor shall His covenant of peace and completeness be removed, because the Lord has compassion on me. (ISAIAH 54:10.)

God is faithful (reliable, trustworthy, and therefore ever true to His promise, and I can depend on Him). (1 CORINTHIANS 1:9.)

Bless (affectionately, gratefully praise) the Lord, O my soul; and all that is [deepest] within me, bless His holy name!

Bless (affectionately, gratefully praise) the Lord, O my soul, and forget not [one of] all His benefits—

Who forgives [every one of] all my iniquities, Who heals [each one of] my diseases,

Who redeems my life from the pit and corruption, Who beautifies, dignifies, and crowns me with loving-kindness and tender mercy. (PSALM 103:1–4.)

The Lord fills my life with good things! My youth is renewed like the eagle's! He gives justice to all who are treated unfairly.

He is merciful and tender toward those who don't deserve it; He is slow to get angry and full of kindness and love. He never bears a grudge, nor remains angry forever for His mercy toward those who fear and honor Him is as great as the height of the heavens above the earth. He has removed my sins as far away from me as the east is from the west. He is like a father to me, tender and sympathetic to me because I reverence Him.

The lovingkindness of the Lord is from everlasting to everlasting. (PSALM 103:5, 6, 8, 9, 11–13, 17 TLB.)

Abiding love surrounds me because I trust in the Lord. (PSALM 32:10 TLB.)

I will praise the Lord no matter what happens. I will constantly speak of His glories and grace. I will boast of all His kindness to me. Let all who are discouraged take heart. Let us praise the Lord together, and exalt His name.

For I cried to Him and He answered me! He freed me from all my fears. Others too were radiant at what He did for them. Theirs was no downcast look of rejection! I cried to the Lord—and the Lord heard me and saved me out of my troubles. For the Angel of the Lord guards and rescues all who reverence Him.

I have put God to the test and have seen how kind He is! I have seen for myself the way His mercies shower down on all who trust in Him. (PSALM 34:1–8 TLB.)

Chapter 2: Your Future

All the days of the desponding and afflicted are made evil [by anxious thoughts and forebodings], but because I have a glad heart I have a continual feast [regardless of my circumstances]. (PROVERBS 15:15.)

[What would have become of me] had I not believed that I would see the Lord's goodness in the land of the living!

I wait and hope for and expect the Lord; I am brave and of good courage and let my heart be stout and enduring. Yes, I wait for and hope for and expect the Lord. (PSALM 27:13, 14.)

I know that the thoughts and plans the Lord has for me are thoughts and plans for welfare and peace and not for evil, to give me hope in my final outcome. (JEREMIAH 29:11.)

Why are you cast down, O my inner self? And why should you moan over me and be disquieted within me? I will hope in God and wait expectantly for Him, for I shall yet praise Him, Who is the help of my countenance, and my God. (PSALM 42:11.)

Such hope never disappoints or deludes or shames me, for God's love has been poured out in my heart through the Holy Spirit Who has been given to me. (ROMANS 5:5.)

The Lord God is a sun and shield: the Lord will give grace and glory: no good thing will he withhold from me because I walk uprightly. (PSALM 84:11 KJV.)

I am convinced and sure of this very thing, that He Who began a good work in me will continue until the day of Jesus Christ [right up to the time of His return], developing [that good work] and perfecting and bringing it to full completion in me. (PHILIPPIANS 1:6.)

I am God's [own] handiwork (His workmanship), re-created in Christ Jesus, [born anew] that I may do those good works which God predestined (planned beforehand) for me [taking paths which He prepared ahead of time], that I should walk in them [living the good life which He prearranged and made ready for me to live]. (EPHESIANS 2:10.)

There is a time [appointed] for every matter and purpose and for every work. Therefore I humble myself under the mighty hand of God that in due time He may exalt me. (ECCLESIASTES 3:17; 1 PETER 5:6.)

The things God plans won't happen right away. Slowly, steadily, surely, the time approaches when the vision will be fulfilled. If it seems slow, I do not despair, for these things will surely come to pass. I will just be patient! They will not be overdue a single day! (HABAKKUK 2:3 TLB.)

I have strong encouragement because I have fled for refuge in laying hold of the hope set before me. This hope I have as an anchor of the soul, a hope both sure and steadfast. (HEBREWS 6:18, 19 NAS.)

I am not afraid for I am assured and know that [God being a partner in my labor] all things work together and are [fitting into a plan] for good to me because I love God and am called according to [His] design and purpose. (ROMANS 8:28.)

My God is able to [carry out His purpose and] do superabundantly, far over and above all that I [dare] ask or think [infinitely beyond my highest prayers, desires, thoughts, hopes, or dreams]. (EPHESIANS 3:20.)

In Jesus Christ I also have been made [God's] heritage (portion) and have obtained an inheritance; for I have been foreordained (chosen and appointed beforehand) in accordance with His purpose, Who works out everything in agreement with the counsel and design of His [own] will. (EPHESIANS 1:11.)

This Book of the Law shall not depart out of my mouth, but I shall meditate on it day and night, that I may observe and do according to all that is written in it. For then I shall make my way prosperous, and then I shall deal wisely and have good success. (JOSHUA 1:8.)

The Word is very near me, in my mouth and in my mind and in my heart, so that I can do it. (DEUTERONOMY 30:14.)

So shall God's Word be that goes forth out of my mouth: it shall not return to Him void [without producing any effect, useless], but it shall accomplish that which He pleases and purposes, and it shall prosper in the thing for which He sent it. (ISAIAH 55:11.)

[Because I], with unveiled face, continue to behold [in the Word of God] as in a mirror the glory of the Lord, I am constantly being transfigured into His very own image in ever increasing splendor and from one degree of glory to another; [for this comes] from the Lord [Who is] the Spirit. (2 CORINTHIANS 3:18.)

I do not conform to this world (this age), [fashioned

after and adapted to its external, superficial customs], but I am transformed (changed) by the [entire] renewal of my mind [by its new ideals and its new attitude], so that I may prove [for myself] what is the good and perfect will of God, even the thing which is good and acceptable and perfect [in His sight for me]. (ROMANS 12:2.)

To me God was pleased to make known how great are the riches of the glory of this mystery, which is Christ within me, the Hope of [realizing the] glory. (COLOSSIANS 1:27.)

Like God, I call those things which be not as though they were, I declare that I am part of a chosen race, a royal priesthood, a dedicated nation, [God's] own purchased, special people, that I may set forth the wonderful deeds and display the virtues and perfections of Him Who called me out of darkness into His marvelous light. (ROMANS 4:17 KJV; 1 PETER 2:9.)

Because I am the Lord's, He will publicly recognize and openly declare me to be His jewel (His special possession, His peculiar treasure), and He will spare me, as a man spares his own son who serves him. (MALACHI 3:17.)

Like the Apostle Paul, I do not consider that I have captured and made it my own [yet]; but one thing I do [it is my one aspiration]: forgetting what lies behind and straining forward to what lies ahead,

I press on toward the goal to win the [supreme and heavenly] prize to which God in Christ Jesus is calling me upward. (PHILIPPIANS 3:13, 14.)

I do not [earnestly] remember the former things; neither do I consider the things of old.

Behold, the Lord is doing a new thing! Now it springs forth; I perceive and know it and give heed to it. He will even make a way for me in the wilderness and rivers of water for me in the desert. (ISAIAH 43:18, 19.)

Because I belong to Him, the Lord blots out and cancels my transgressions, for His own sake, and He will not remember my sins. (ISAIAH 43:25.)

Because I wait for the Lord [expect, look for, and hope in Him] I shall change and renew my strength and power; I shall lift my wings and mount up [close to God] as eagles [mount up to the sun]; I shall run and not be weary, I shall walk and not faint or become tired. (ISAIAH 40:31.)

I am fully satisfied and assured that God is able and mighty to keep His Word and to do what He has promised me, because I have a divine destiny to fulfill. (ROMANS 4:21.)

Chapter 3: Your Righteousness in Christ

For my sake God made Christ [virtually] to be sin Who knew no sin, so that in and through Him I might become [endued with, viewed as being in, and an example of] the righteousness of God [what I ought to be, approved and acceptable and in right relationship with Him, by His goodness]. (2 CORINTHIANS 5:21.)

As is Your name, O God, so is Your praise to the ends of the earth; Your right hand is full of righteousness [rightness and justice]. (PSALM 48:10.)

And He will establish me to the end [keep me steadfast, give me strength, and guarantee my vindication; He will be my warrant against all accusation or indictment so that I will be] guiltless and irreproachable in the day of our Lord Jesus Christ (the Messiah). (1 CORINTHIANS 1:8)

Blessed and fortunate and happy and spiritually prosperous (in that state in which the born-again child of God enjoys His favor and salvation) am I who hunger and thirst for righteousness (uprightness and right standing with God), for I shall be completely satisfied! (MATTHEW 5:6.)

I cast my burden on the Lord [releasing the weight of

it] and He will sustain me; He will never allow the [consistently] righteous to be moved (made to slip, fall, or fail). (PSALM 55:22.)

The Bible was written for my sake too, to let me know that [righteousness, standing acceptable to God] will be granted and credited to me also for I believe in (trust in, adhere to, and rely on) God, Who raised Jesus my Lord from the dead. (ROMANS 4:24.)

Therefore, since I am justified (acquitted, declared righteous, and given a right standing with God) through faith, I grasp [the fact that I] have [the peace of reconciliation to hold and to enjoy] peace with God through my Lord Jesus Christ (the Messiah, the Anointed One). (ROMANS 5:1.)

Because I am a righteous person I walk in my integrity; blessed (happy, fortunate, enviable) are my children after me. (PROVERBS 20:7.)

Because I am [consistently] righteous, my salvation is of the Lord; He is my Refuge and secure Stronghold in the time of trouble. (PSALM 37:39.)

No weapon that is formed against me shall prosper, and every tongue that shall rise against me in judgment I shall show to be in the wrong. This [peace, righteousness, security, triumph over opposition] is my heritage as a servant of the Lord [in whom the ideal Servant of the Lord is reproduced]; this is the righteousness or the vindication which I obtain from Him [this is that which He imparts to me as my justification]. (ISAIAH 54:17.)

Because I am [uncompromisingly] righteous, the eyes of the Lord are toward me and His ears are open to my cry.

When I, the righteous, cry for help, the Lord hears, and delivers me out of all my distress and troubles.

Many evils confront me, the [consistently] righteous, but the Lord delivers me out of them all.

Because I am the Lord's servant, He redeems my life; I take refuge and trust in Him, and I shall not be condemned or held guilty. (PSALM 34:15, 17, 19, 22.)

I shall establish myself in righteousness (rightness, in conformity with God's will and order): I shall be far from even the thought of oppression or destruction, for I shall not fear, and from terror, for it shall not come near me. (ISAIAH 54:14.)

Because I am [uncompromisingly] righteous, I am as bold as a lion. (PROVERBS 28:1.)

I do not have a High Priest Who is unable to understand and sympathize and have a shared feeling with my weaknesses and infirmities and liability to the assaults of temptation, but One Who has been tempted in every respect as I am, yet without sinning.

I then fearlessly and confidently and boldly draw near to the throne of grace (the throne of God's unmerited favor to me), that I may receive mercy [for my failures] and find grace to help in good time for every need [appropriate help and well-timed help, coming just when I need it]. (HEBREWS 4:15, 16.)

Therefore, since I am now justified (acquitted, made righteous, and brought into right relationship with God) by Christ's blood, how much more [certain is it that] I shall be saved by Him from the indignation and wrath of God. (ROMANS 5:9.)

Blessed (happy, fortunate, prosperous, and enviable) am I because I walk and live not in the counsel of the ungodly [following their advice, their plans and purposes], nor stand [submissive and inactive] in the path where sinners walk, nor sit down [to relax and rest] where the scornful [and the mockers] gather.

But my delight and desire are in the law of the Lord, and on His law (the precepts, the instructions, the teachings of God) I habitually meditate (ponder and study) by day and by night.

And I shall be like a tree firmly planted [and tended] by the streams of water, ready to bring forth fruit in season; my leaf also shall not fade or wither, and everything I do shall prosper [and come to maturity]. (PSALM 1:1–3.)

This Book of the Law shall not depart out of my mouth, but I shall meditate on it day and night that I may observe and do according to all that is written in it. For then I shall make my way prosperous, and then I shall deal wisely and have good success. (JOSHUA 1:8.)

The name of the Lord is a strong tower; as a [consistently] righteous person [upright and in right standing with God], I run into it and am safe, high [above evil] and strong. (PROVERBS 18:10.)

In His [Christ's] day shall I, the [uncompromisingly] righteous, flourish and my peace shall abound until there is a moon no longer. (PSALM 72:7.)

This is the agreement (testament, covenant) that God has set up with me: He has imprinted His laws upon my heart and has inscribed them upon my mind (on my inmost thoughts and understanding).

My sins and lawbreaking He remembers no more.

Now since there is absolute remission (forgiveness and cancellation of the penalty) of my [sins and lawbreaking], I no longer have to make any offering to atone for them. (HEBREWS 10:16–18.)

I have full freedom and confidence to enter into the [Holy of] Holies [by the power and virtue] in the blood of Jesus,

By this fresh (new) and living way which He initiated and dedicated and opened for me through the separating curtain (veil of the Holy of Holies), that is, through His flesh. (HEBREWS 10:19, 20.)

For my sake God made Christ [virtually] to be sin Who knew no sin, so that in and through Him I might become [endued with, viewed as being, and an example of] the righteousness of God [what I ought to be, approved and acceptable and in right relationship with Him, by His goodness]. (2 CORINTHIANS 5:21.)

Chapter 4: Overcoming Fear

For God did not give me a spirit of timidity (of cowardice, of craven and cringing and fawning fear), but [He has given me a spirit] of power and of love and calm and well-balanced mind and discipline and self-control. (2 TIMOTHY 1:7.)

I sought (inquired of) the Lord and required Him [of necessity and on the authority of His Word], and He heard me, and delivered me from all my fears. (PSALM 34:4.)

I do not let my heart be troubled, neither do I let it be afraid. [I stop allowing myself to be agitated and disturbed; and I do not permit myself to be fearful and intimidated and cowardly and unsettled]. (JOHN 14:27.)

What time I am afraid, I will have confidence in and put my trust and reliance in the Lord.

By [the help of] God I will praise His Word; on God I lean, rely, and confidently put my trust; I will not fear. What can man, who is flesh, do to me? (PSALM 56:3, 4.)

[There is nothing to fear], for God is with me; I do not look around me in terror or become dismayed, for He is my God. He will strengthen and harden me to difficulties, yes, He will help me; yes, He will hold me up and retain me with His [victorious] right hand of rightness and justice. (ISAIAH 41:10.)

[God] Himself has said, I will not in any way fail you nor give you up nor leave you without support. **[I will]**

not, [I will] not, [I will] not in any degree leave you helpless nor forsake nor let [you] down (relax My hold on you)! [Assuredly not!]

So I take comfort and am encouraged and confidently and boldly say, The Lord is my Helper; I will not be seized with alarm [I will not fear or dread or be terrified]. What can man do to me? (HEBREWS 13:5, 6.)

The Lord my God holds my right hand; He is the Lord, Who says to me, Fear not; I will help you! (ISAIAH 41:13.)

I am not afraid for I am assured and know that [God being a partner in my labor] all things work together and are [fitting into a plan] for good to me because I love God and am called according to [His] design and purpose. (ROMANS 8:28.)

The Lord who created me says, Don't be afraid, for I have ransomed you; I have called you by name; you are Mine. When you go through deep waters and great trouble, I will be with you. When you go through rivers of difficulty, you will not drown! When you walk through the fire of oppression, you will not be burned up—the flames will not consume you. For I am the Lord your God, your Savior, the Holy one of Israel. (ISAIAH 43:1–3 TLB.)

I will not be afraid, because fear has torment.

Instead, I dare to have the boldness (courage and confidence) of free access (an unreserved approach to God with freedom and without fear).

So I do not lose heart [nor faint or become despondent through fear]. (1 JOHN 4:18 KJV; EPHESIANS 3:12, 13.)

God is my Refuge and Strength [mighty and impenetrable to temptation], a very present and well-proved help in trouble.

Therefore I will not fear, though the earth should change and though the mountains be shaken into the midst of the seas. (PSALM 46:1, 2.)

I will be strong, vigorous, and very courageous. I will not be afraid, neither will I be dismayed, for the Lord my God is with me wherever I go. (JOSHUA 1:9.)

I will not be afraid; the Lord's eye is upon me because I fear Him [revere and worship Him with awe], because I wait for Him and hope in His mercy and lovingkindness. (PSALM 33:18.)

I do not worry and am not anxious about tomorrow, for tomorrow will have worries and anxieties of its own. Sufficient for each day is its own trouble. (MATTHEW 6:34.)

I do not fear because I will no longer live in shame. The shame of my youth and the sorrows of widowhood will be remembered no more, for my Creator will be my "husband." The Lord of Hosts is His name; He is my Redeemer, the Holy One of Israel, the God of all the earth. (ISAIAH 54:4 TLB.)

When I am tempted to have a fearful and hasty heart, I say to myself, Be strong, fear not! Behold, your God will come with vengeance; with His recompense He will come and save you. (ISAIAH 35:4.)

I am not afraid because God has granted me out of the rich treasury of His glory to be strengthened and reinforced with mighty power in the inner man by the [Holy] Spirit [Himself indwelling my innermost being and personality]. (EPHESIANS 3:16.)

I will praise the Lord and exalt His name for I cried to Him and He answered me! He freed me from all my fears. (PSALM 34:3, 4 TLB.)

I am not afraid for there is no fear in love [dread does not exist], but full-grown (complete, perfect) love turns fear out of doors and expels every trace of terror! For fear brings with it the thought of punishment. I do not fear because I have reached the full maturity of love [have grown into love's complete perfection]. (1 JOHN 4:18.)

The Lord is my Light and my Salvation; whom shall I fear? When evil men come to destroy me, they will stumble and fall! Yes, though a mighty army marches against me, my heart shall know no fear! I am confident that God will save me.

When trouble comes, the Lord will hide me. He will set me on a high rock out of reach of all my enemies. Then I will bring Him sacrifices and sing His praises with much joy. (PSALM 27:1–3, 5, 6 TLB.)

I will not fear, for from the first day that I set my mind and heart to understand and to humble myself before my God, my words were heard, and God has sent His angel as a consequence of [and in response to] my words. (DANIEL 10:12.)

When I am brought to trial before rulers and authorities, I will not be concerned about what to say in my defense, for the Holy Spirit will give me the right words even as I am standing there. (LUKE 12:11 TLB.)

The Lord is my Shepherd; I shall not want.

He makes me lie down in green pastures: He leads me beside the still waters.

He restores my soul: He leads me in the paths of righteousness for His name's sake.

Though I walk through the valley of the shadow of death, I will fear no evil: for the Lord is with me; His rod and His staff they comfort me.

He prepares a table before me in the presence of my enemies: He anoints my head with oil; my cup runs over.

Surely goodness and mercy shall follow me all the days of my life: and I will dwell in the house of the Lord forever. (PSALM 23:1–6 KJV.)

Conclusion: Standing Fast

I will stand fast therefore in the liberty wherewith Christ has made me free, and I will not be entangled again with the yoke of bondage. (GALATIANS 5:1 KJV.)

I will not fling away my fearless confidence, for it carries a great and glorious compensation of reward.

For I have need of steadfast patience and endurance, so that I may perform and fully accomplish the will of God, and thus receive and carry away [and enjoy to the full] what is promised to me. (HEBREWS 10:35, 36.)

REFERENCES

Scripture quotations marked (KJV) are taken from the *King James Version* of the Bible.

Scripture quotations marked (TLB) are taken from *The Living Bible* © 1971. Used by permission of Tyndale House Publishers, Inc., Wheaton, Illinois 60189. All rights reserved.

Scripture quotations marked (NAS) are taken from the *New American Standard Bible.* Copyright © The Lockman Foundation 1960, 1962, 1963, 1968, 1971, 1972, 1973, 1975, 1977. Used by permission.

ABOUT THE AUTHOR

❦

JOYCE MEYER has been teaching the scriptures since 1976 and in full-time ministry since 1980. She is the bestselling author of over 54 inspirational books, including *Secrets to Exceptional Living, The Joy of Believing Prayer,* and *Battlefield of the Mind,* as well as over 220 audiocassette albums and over 90 videos. Joyce's *Life in the Word* radio and television programs are broadcast around the world, and she travels extensively to share her message in her popular "Life in the Word" conferences. Joyce and her husband Dave are the parents of four children and make their home in St. Louis, Missouri.

To contact the author write:

Joyce Meyer Ministries
P. O. Box 655
Fenton, Missouri 63026
or call: (636) 349-0303
Internet Address: www.joycemeyer.org

*Please include your testimony or help received from this book
when you write. Your prayer requests are welcome.*

To contact the author
in Canada, please write:
Joyce Meyer Ministries Canada, Inc.
Lambeth Box 1300
London, ON N6P 1T5
or call: (636) 349-0303

In Australia, please write:
Joyce Meyer Ministries-Australia
Locked Bag 77
Mansfield Delivery Centre
Queensland 4122
or call: 07 3349 1200

In England, please write:
Joyce Meyer Ministries
P. O. Box 1549
Windsor
SL4 1GT
Or call: (0) 1753-831102

Joyce Meyer Titles